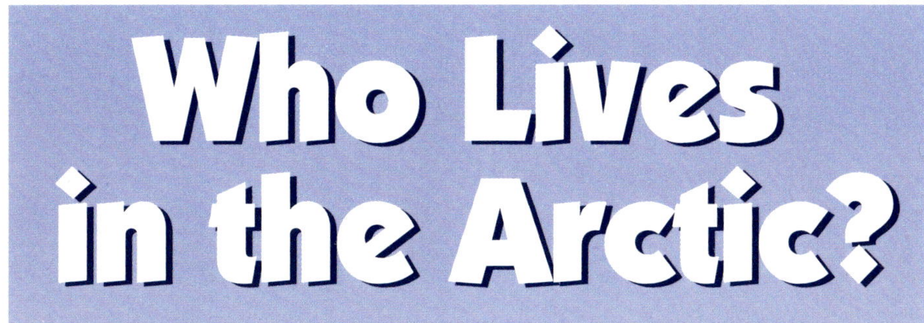

Who Lives in the Arctic?

Susan Canizares • Pamela Chanko

Scholastic Inc.

New York • Toronto • London • Auckland • Sydney

Acknowledgments

Science Consultants: Patrick R. Thomas, Ph.D., Bronx Zoo/Wildlife Conservation Park; Glenn Phillips, The New York Botanical Garden; **Literacy Specialist:** Maria Utefsky, Reading Recovery Coordinator, District 2, New York City

Design: MKR Design, Inc.

Photo Research: Barbara Scott

Endnotes: Susan Russell

Photographs: Cover: M. P. Kahl/DRK Photo; p. 1: Stephen J. Krasemann/DRK Photo; p. 2: Fred Bruemmer/Peter Arnold; p. 3: Johnny Johnson/DRK Photo; p. 4: Louis Gagnon/Animals, Animals; p. 5: Jim Brandenburg/Minden Pictures; p. 6: Johnny Johnson/DRK Photo; p. 7: Wayne Lankinen/DRK Photo; p. 8: Stephen J. Krasemann/DRK Photo; p. 9: Tom & Pat Leeson/DRK Photo; p. 10: Fred Bruemmer/DRK Photo; p. 11: Jim Brandenburg/Minden Pictures; p. 12: Lawrence Migdale.

Library of Congress Cataloging-in-Publication Data
Canizares, Susan, 1960-
Who lives in the Arctic? / Susan Canizares, Pamela Chanko.
p. cm. -- (Science emergent readers)
"Scholastic early childhood."
Includes index.
Summary: Photographs and simple text explore the variety of animals that have adapted to life in the Arctic.
ISBN 0-590-76150-1 (pbk.: alk. paper)
1. Zoology--Arctic regions--Juvenile literature. [1. Zoology--Arctic regions.]
I. Chanko, Pamela, 1968-. II. Title. III. Series.
QL105.C358 1998
591.998--dc21 97-34202
CIP AC

Printed in the U.S.A.
3 4 5 6 7 8 9 10 03 02 01 00 99 98

Who lives in the Arctic?

Seals live in the Arctic.

Whales do, too.

Moose live in the Arctic.

Reindeer do, too.

Grizzly bears live in the Arctic.

Polar bears do, too.

Foxes live in the Arctic.

Hares do, too.

Musk oxen live in the Arctic.

Wolves live in the Arctic.

People do, too!

Who Lives in the Arctic?

The Arctic is a vast area made up of land and sea surrounding the North Pole. The weather in the Arctic is extremely cold. Most of the Arctic Ocean is covered with ice floes year round, and the land is often buried under snow and ice. During the winter it is dark most of the time. Despite these harsh conditions many mammals, birds, and fish are able to survive and thrive in this environment.

The Arctic Ocean is rich with marine life. Seals, like the Harp Seals (left), feed on the abundant fish. There are about 10 species of seals living in the Arctic. The whales (right) also eat fish, squid, and sometimes plankton. They can live in the cold water because of a thick layer of blubber that keeps them warm.

The Moose (left) is the largest member of the deer family. It grazes on willow and migrates seasonally in order to find it. The Reindeer (right) burrows under the snow to find the lichen it feeds on. Both the moose and the reindeer have antlers that are shed and regrown each year. And both these animals are the prey of wolves.

Grizzly Bears (left) forage for food on the tundra, the Arctic land. They eat everything from berries and roots to small animals and fish. Polar Bears (right) live on the ice floes and hunt seals for food. Both kinds of bears hibernate, sleeping in dens throughout the winter.

The coat of the Arctic Fox (left) changes from winter white to summer brown. This small, quick hunter's range extends from the ice, where it eats leftover seal meat, to the wilderness, where it hunts small animals. Like the fox, the Snowshoe Hare (right) has a white coat in winter and a brown one in summer.

The Muskoxen (left) live in herds and have adapted well to the Arctic environment, eating the few grasses that are available. Their horns are not shed like antlers. They are also the prey of the Arctic Wolf (right). Wolves are meat-eating animals and range over large territories, hunting in packs. Wolves stay with one mate, which is rare in the animal kingdom.